A Journey
HOME

Printed in the United States of America.

Library of Congress Control Number: 2019910109

ISBN   Paperback   978-1-64361-789-3
               Hardback   978-1-64361-790-9
               eBook   978-1-64361-791-6

Westwood Books Publishing LLC
10389 Almayo Ave, Suite 103
Los Angeles, CA 90064

www.westwoodbookspublishing.com

A Journey
HOME

Teaching a child about loss of a loved one

ALYCIA R. WRIGHT

This book is dedicated to the dearest and the kindest of families. The McGee's who opened their hearts and home to entrust his care to me. To share completely in their house of love at such a delicate and trying time was an honor. Matthew now has his wings!

I met a boy named Matthew.
His hair was light-brown-gold.
Everywhere that Matthew went,
angels were sure to follow.

1

His huge brown eyes, so innocent!
His laugh was sure to please.
Matthew's family was warm and sensitive.
They could place anyone at ease.

2

He followed me to my home one day.
In my thoughts, his heart—so sweet.
I may have never met him,
except for fate's necessity.

3

I am a nurse and he is a child.
A special bond we keep.
I sit beside his bed each night,
to watch while he is asleep.

4

It is by touch that we communicated.
No time for feeling sad.
Our spirits had connected,
on those quiet nights we sat.

5

That Matthew was a special boy.
Best of both worlds has he!
All comfy nestled in his bed;
yet, a spirit that flies free.

6

7

He tells me things I would never know.
If listen I had not intend.
A precious gift named Matthew,
did God so circumvent.

He says that he will miss you.
Matt knows how sad we will be,
when he will wander off one day,
to spend eternity.

In eternity he will romp and play.
He will endure sickness no more.
There, he will begin an everlasting life,
and suffer no pain like before.

Matthew sends his love and wishes to say,
he knows you really care.
It is just that God has called him.
To come and climb His stairs.

9

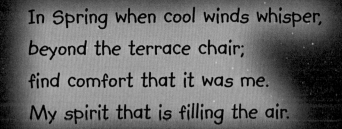

In Spring when cool winds whisper,
beyond the terrace chair;
find comfort that it was me.
My spirit that is filling the air.

"Fret not for me.
I know it is hard,
To let go of good times.
Keep loving memories in your heart,
with thoughts of me from time to time."
"Remember that I love you.
I am sorry I could not stay."
Said Matthew in a whisper,
the night he went away.